Complete Diabetic Renal Diet Cookbook For Over 40

Nourish Your Body, Protect Your Kidneys, and Manage Diabetes with Flavorful Recipes

Mill V. Mike

Copyright © 2024, Mill V. Mike

Table of Content

Introduction To Diabetic Renal Diet Cookbook For Over 40

Go with me on a journey through the pages of "Complete Diabetic Renal Diet Cookbook For Over 40, a culmination of my expedition through the intricate dance of flavors, nutrition, and health management. As a chef deeply immersed in the world of culinary arts and a passionate advocate for healthy living, I've always been fascinated by the power of food. Food is not just sustenance; it's a medicine, a comfort, and a way of life. This book is born from my years of experience, research, and heartfelt conversations with people navigating the complexities of managing both diabetes and kidney health as they step into the vibrant stage of life after 40.

Entering the fourth decade of life brings unique challenges and rewards. It's a time when our bodies begin to whisper (sometimes shout) the consequences of our lifelong habits. For those of us managing diabetes and renal health, the whispers can seem daunting. But here's the thing: with the right knowledge, tools, and mindset, it's not just possible to live well; it's possible to thrive.

This cookbook is more than just a collection of recipes; it's a guide to understanding how each ingredient affects your blood sugar, your kidneys, and overall health. It's about learning to balance the delicate equation of nutrition and flavor, ensuring that every meal is not only a joy to the palate but also a building block for your health.

As we embark on this journey together, I invite you to bring an open mind, a willing heart, and a hungry stomach. We'll explore the science behind the diabetic renal diet, debunk myths, and arm ourselves with practical knowledge to make informed choices. From the grocery store aisles to the kitchen counters, we'll navigate the challenges of meal planning, shopping, and cooking in a way that's both enjoyable and sustainable.

The recipes you'll discover here are designed with love, care, and a deep understanding of the nutritional needs of individuals over 40 managing both diabetes and renal health. They are a testament to the fact that dietary restrictions do not mean a compromise on taste or variety. Whether you're a seasoned chef or someone who's just beginning to explore the kitchen, there's something in here for you.

This book is my invitation to you: to rediscover the joy of cooking and eating, to embrace the transformative power of food, and to celebrate the journey towards better health. Together, let's turn the page and start this delicious adventure.

The Intersection of Diabetes and Renal Health After 40

Navigating the intersection of diabetes and renal health after 40 is akin to walking a tightrope a delicate balance between what nourishes and what harms. As we cross into the later chapters of our lives, our bodies whisper (and sometimes shout) the need for a pivotal shift towards mindful nutrition and lifestyle changes. This is where knowledge, seasoned with the zest of culinary artistry, transforms from mere information to a powerful tool for self-empowerment.

Imagine standing at the crossroads of tradition and innovation in your kitchen. Here, the pots and pans aren't just utensils; they're instruments of change. The ingredients? Not just food, but medicine that heals and fortifies. For those of us navigating the complexities of managing diabetes and renal health after 40, the equation isn't just about subtraction eliminating this, reducing that, but about addiction. Adding joy, flavor, and color to our plates and, by extension, our lives.

Empowering Yourself Through Knowledge and Cuisine

Crafting meals that cater to both diabetic and renal health requirements doesn't mean a life sentence of blandness or monotony. On the contrary, it opens up a canvas for creativity a challenge to reinvent and reimagine the way we eat. It's about understanding the science behind each ingredient's impact on our blood sugar and kidneys, and then applying that knowledge with the flair of a seasoned chef. This culinary journey isn't just about adhering to a list of dietary restrictions; it's about embracing a lifestyle that prioritizes wellness without sacrificing pleasure.

The narrative often peddled in the mainstream can paint a grim picture, suggesting that a diagnosis of diabetes or renal issues is the end of culinary enjoyment. But let's flip the script. Let's dive into the vibrant world of herbs, spices, and nutrient-rich foods that not only cater to our health needs but also tantalize your taste buds. It's about crafting dishes that bring people together, dishes that spark conversation and delight in every bite because, at its heart, food is about connection, celebration, and love.

In the "Complete Diabetic Renal Diet Cookbook For Over 40," we embark on a journey together, a journey of transformation. Through these pages, you'll discover not just recipes, but a new perspective on food and health. You'll learn that each meal is an opportunity to nourish not just your body, but also your soul. This book is a testament to the power of food as a vehicle for healing, joy, and discovery.

As we delve into the chapters, we'll explore the science behind food choices, unravel the myths, and build a foundation of knowledge that empowers you to make informed decisions. From the market to the kitchen, from the stove to the table, every step is an integral part of the journey towards a healthier, happier you.

Remember, embracing a diet that supports both diabetes and renal health after 40 isn't about restrictions, it's about liberation. It's about breaking free from the cycle of unhealthy choices and stepping into a world where food becomes your ally in health. So, let's turn the page and begin this culinary adventure together, one delicious, healthful meal at a time.

Chapter 1:

Understanding the Diabetic Renal Diet

In the kitchen of life, where health is the main ingredient, understanding the diabetic renal diet is akin to mastering the art of seasoning. A little knowledge goes a long way in enhancing the flavor of your daily existence. Let's embark on a journey through the biology of kidney health and uncover the nutritional strategies that serve as the backbone of managing both blood sugar and renal function.

1.1 The Biology of Diabetes and Kidney Health

Imagine your kidneys as the body's most diligent chefs, working tirelessly behind the scenes. These bean-shaped wonders filter out waste, balance electrolytes, and manage blood pressure. They're the unsung heroes in the narrative of your body's health, especially so when managing diabetes.

However, when diabetes enters the scene, it's like a persistent kitchen mishap, where sugar (glucose) builds up in the bloodstream, turning what should be a source of energy into a potential saboteur. Over time, high blood sugar can cause a traffic jam in the kidney's filtration system, leading to chronic kidney disease (CKD). The goal, then, is to manage this delicate balance, ensuring the kidneys don't bear the brunt of diabetes' impact.

1.2 Nutritional Strategies for Managing Blood Sugar and Renal Function

Navigating your diet with these considerations in mind is crucial. It's not merely about avoiding sugar and salt; it's about creating a symphony of nutrients that supports both your blood sugar levels and your kidneys. Here's how:

Control Blood Sugar: Focus on low-glycemic foods such as those that keep your blood sugar levels steady.

Low-glycemic foods include:
Whole Grains: Think beyond white bread to nutrient-rich alternatives like barley, bulgur, and farro. These grains are not only flavorful but also packed with fiber, which slows down the absorption of sugar.

Legumes: Beans, lentils, and chickpeas are not only low in glycemic index but also high in protein and fiber, making them a powerhouse of nutrition and a staple for any health-conscious kitchen.

Non-Starchy Vegetables: Leafy greens, broccoli, and peppers add color, texture, and a host of vitamins and minerals to your plate, all while keeping your blood sugar in check.

Some Fruits: While fruits are an essential part of a balanced diet, choosing those with a lower glycemic index, such as berries, cherries, and apples, can help manage blood sugar levels more effectively.

Reduce Sodium: Excessive salt is a burden on the kidneys. Imagine sodium as an overzealous cook who overwhelms a dish. Instead, flavor your meals with herbs and spices, such as cinnamon, fenugreek seeds, turmeric, garlic, parsley, dill, cilantro, paprika, black pepper, and cardamom. By doing so, you're not only enhancing the flavor of your meals but also taking a proactive step towards managing your blood sugar and supporting your kidneys, all while enjoying the rich tapestry of tastes that herbs and spices bring to your table.

Monitor Protein Intake: While protein is a cornerstone of a healthy diet, excessive amounts can strain the kidneys. Picture your protein sources as part of a balanced ensemble, not the solo act.

Limit Phosphorus and Potassium: Certain nutrients, like phosphorus and potassium, require careful management in a renal diet. They're like ingredients that only need to be used sparingly, to not overpower the dish.

Stay Hydrated: Water is the essence of life and a key player in kidney health. Think of it as the oil that keeps the machinery running smoothly, flushing out toxins and keeping everything in balance.

The journey to mastering the diabetic renal diet is not a solitary endeavor. It's a shared culinary adventure where knowledge empowers, food heals, and every meal is a step toward wellness. Together, let's transform the narrative of health through the power of nutrition, one delicious, life-affirming bite at a time.

Chapter 2:

Nutrients in Focus

2.1 Key Nutrients for the Diabetic Renal Diet

Understanding the key nutrients essential for your diet is like navigating a map to treasure. It's not just about what to avoid; it's about discovering the wealth of foods that can enrich your health. This guide aims to illuminate the path with practical advice, ensuring your journey is both enjoyable and beneficial.

Proteins: The Balancing Act
Proteins are vital for repairing tissues and maintaining muscle mass, but it's crucial to get the balance right. Opt for high-quality sources like fish, chicken, and plant-based proteins such as lentils and chickpeas. These

choices help maintain muscle health without overburdening the kidneys.

Carbohydrates: Choose Wisely
Carbohydrates are your body's primary energy source, but choosing the right types makes all the difference. Pay attention to the complex carbs that are present in fruits, vegetables, and whole grains. These not only provide sustained energy but also come packed with fiber, aiding in blood sugar regulation.

Fats: The Good Kind
Not all fats are created equal. Embrace monounsaturated and polyunsaturated fats from sources like olive oil, nuts, and avocados. These fats support heart health—an important consideration given the increased heart disease risk associated with diabetes and kidney issues.

Sodium: Less is More
Sodium can be a foe in managing blood pressure and kidney health. Use herbs and

spices to flavor food instead of salt. This simple swap can have a profound impact on your health, reducing the risk of hypertension and kidney strain.

Potassium and Phosphorus: Keep in Check
Monitoring potassium and phosphorus intake is key. Opt for fruits and vegetables low in potassium and consume phosphorus-rich foods in moderation. Your diet doesn't have to be restrictive; it's about making informed choices that support your health goals.

Water: The Essence of Life
Hydration plays a critical role in kidney health. Water helps flush out toxins, aiding your kidneys in their filtration process. Aim for clear urine as a sign of proper hydration, adjusting intake based on your healthcare provider's recommendations.

Crafting Your Diet
Incorporating these nutrients into your diet isn't just about adhering to a list of do's and

don'ts; it's about crafting a lifestyle that celebrates food as a source of nourishment and joy. Experiment with recipes that emphasize these key nutrients, finding joy in the flavors and satisfaction in the health benefits they bring.

2.2 Understanding and Managing Potassium, Phosphorus, and Sodium Intake

In the culinary journey of managing diabetes and renal health, understanding and managing your intake of potassium, phosphorus, and sodium becomes a crucial chapter. It's not merely about restriction; it's about making informed choices that enhance both the quality and enjoyment of your meals. Let's delve into practical strategies for balancing these key minerals, ensuring your diet supports your health without sacrificing flavor.

Potassium: The Art of Balance
Potassium plays a pivotal role in maintaining nerve function and muscle

health, including the heart. But, when it comes to kidney health, balance is key. Too much potassium can be problematic, yet it's found in many fruits and vegetables. The solution? Choose lower-potassium options like apples, berries, and green beans, and be mindful of portion sizes. Cooking methods like boiling can also help reduce potassium content in vegetables.

Phosphorus: The Hidden Challenge
Phosphorus, essential for bone health, becomes a mineral to watch due to its impact on kidneys and bone health when levels in the blood are too high. It's stealthily present in many foods, especially processed ones, making label reading a critical skill. Opt for fresh, whole foods and limit foods with "phos" additives to manage your phosphorus intake effectively.

Sodium: Flavor without the Salt
Sodium is notorious for its role in hypertension, a common concern for those managing diabetes and kidney health. The

key to reducing sodium intake isn't to sacrifice flavor but to find alternative ways to season your food. Herbs, spices, lemon juice, and vinegar can all add zest to your dishes without the need for salt. Also, cooking at home allows you to control the sodium content, making it easier to enjoy delicious meals that are kind to your kidneys and heart.

Practical Tips for Daily Eating
Read Labels: Become a detective in the grocery store, looking out for sodium and phosphorus content, especially in packaged foods.

Choose Fresh: Fresh fruits, vegetables, and meats are naturally lower in these minerals compared to their processed counterparts.

Cook Smart: Use cooking methods that help reduce potassium in vegetables and always opt for herbs and spices over salt.

Portion Control: Even with lower-potassium foods, keeping an eye on portions ensures you don't inadvertently consume too much.
Consultation: Working with a dietitian can provide personalized advice tailored to your specific health needs and dietary restrictions.

Understanding and managing your intake of potassium, phosphorus, and sodium doesn't mean you have to compromise on taste or enjoyment. It all comes down to making more informed decisions that improve your general health as well as your taste buds. Armed with knowledge and creativity, you can continue to enjoy meals that are as nourishing as they are delightful, supporting your health journey every step of the way.

Chapter 3:

Decoding Food Labels

Navigating the supermarket aisles can feel like trying to decipher an ancient script. Food labels, with their small print and long lists of ingredients, can be perplexing. Yet, understanding them is crucial to managing diabetes and renal health, as well as spotting hidden sugars, sodium, and unhealthy fats. This chapter aims to simplify this task, turning the complex into something straightforward and manageable.

The Basics of Food Labels

At first glance, food labels provide a summary of the nutritional value of a product. Start with the serving size, located at the top. It's the key to understanding the rest of the information. This quantity serves as the basis for all of the nutritional information given below. It's common for packages to contain more than one serving, so adjust your calculations accordingly

3.1 A Guide to Making Informed Choices

Armed with knowledge, making healthier choices becomes simpler. Opt for fresh or minimally processed foods whenever possible, as these are less likely to contain hidden sugars, excessive sodium, or unhealthy fats. When choosing packaged foods, use the label to guide you to the best options for your health.

Practical Tips for Everyday Shopping
Start with the Serving Size: Adjust your intake based on the actual amount you eat.

Check for Sugars: Look beyond "sugars" to find hidden sources.

Monitor Sodium: Opt for low-sodium options to protect your heart and kidneys.

Identify Fats: Choose products low in saturated and trans fats.

Decoding food labels doesn't have to be a daunting task. With these guidelines, you're equipped to make choices that align with your health goals, simplifying the path to wellness. Remember, every informed choice is a step towards better health and well-being.

3.2 Spotting Hidden Sugars, Sodium, and Unhealthy Fats

Sugars have many disguises and can appear under various names: fructose, glucose, sucrose, maltose, lactose, dextrose, and high-fructose corn syrup, to name a few. Keep an eye out for these terms, especially in products that may not even taste sweet, like bread and condiments. Remember, sugars contribute to blood sugar spikes and can be particularly harmful in a diabetic diet.

Sodium: Less Is More
Sodium is often added to processed foods not only for flavor but also as a preservative.

High sodium intake is linked to hypertension and can be challenging for kidney health. The recommended daily limit is less than 2,300 mg, but lower is better, especially for those with health concerns. When looking at labels, choose products with lower sodium content, aiming for those that provide 5% Daily Value (DV) or less per serving.

Unhealthy Fats: What to Avoid

It's important to avoid trans and saturated fats. Trans fats, often listed as "partially hydrogenated oils," are particularly harmful and should be avoided as much as possible. Saturated fats, found in animal products and some oils, should be limited. Instead, look for foods high in monounsaturated and polyunsaturated fats, which support heart health.

Chapter 4:

Meal Planning and Preparation

Embarking on a healthful eating journey doesn't have to be a daunting task, especially with a bit of planning and the right tools at your disposal. This chapter is your guide to structuring daily meals, incorporating time-saving strategies, and identifying essential kitchen tools that make healthy cooking both achievable and enjoyable.

4.1 Structuring Your Daily Meal Plan

Structuring Your Daily Meal Plan
A well-structured meal plan is the cornerstone of managing diabetes and renal health. The goal is to balance your intake of proteins, carbohydrates, and fats, while also considering the nuances of potassium, phosphorus, and sodium.

Breakfast: Start with a protein-rich meal paired with complex carbohydrates to kickstart your metabolism and maintain stable blood sugar levels. Think of an omelet with veggies or a bowl of steel-cut oats topped with nuts.

Lunch: Focus on lean protein and a variety of vegetables to keep you full and energized. A quinoa salad with grilled chicken or a vegetable stir-fry with tofu can be perfect.

Dinner: Aim for lighter fare that's easy on the kidneys. Fish or lean poultry with a side of steamed vegetables and a small portion of whole grains works well.

Snacks: Choose snacks that support blood sugar balance, like a small handful of almonds or a piece of fruit with a slice of cheese.

4.2 Time-Saving Tips and Techniques for Busy Lives

Preparing meals from scratch daily can be challenging, but a few strategies can make it more manageable:

Batch Cooking: Prepare and cook large portions of meals at once, then store them in the fridge or freezer. This approach is especially useful for grains, proteins, and soups.

Prep in Advance: Spend some time washing and chopping vegetables, marinating proteins, or assembling salads in jars after your grocery run. This makes putting meals together much quicker.

Use Leftovers Creatively: Transform leftovers into new meals to save time and reduce waste. Yesterday's grilled chicken can become today's chicken salad.

4.3 Essential Kitchen Tools for Healthy Cooking

Having the right tools can make healthy cooking more efficient and enjoyable. Consider these essentials:

Sharp Knives: A good set of knives can make meal prep faster and safer. Purchasing a serrated knife, paring knife, and chef's knife is a wise investment. Food Processor: This versatile tool can save time on chopping, grating, and blending, making it easier to prepare dishes in bulk.

Slow Cooker or Pressure Cooker: These appliances are excellent for making healthy meals with minimal effort. They can tenderize less expensive cuts of meat and cook beans or whole grains perfectly.

Non-Stick Skillet and Pots: Quality cookware is crucial for healthy cooking, allowing you to use less oil.

Measuring Cups and Spoons: Accurate measurements help manage portion sizes and ingredient ratios, essential for keeping track of macronutrient intake.

Chapter 5:

Kitchens Are the Heart of the Home

The kitchen is not just a room; it's a gathering place, a laboratory for creativity, and most importantly, the heart of a health-conscious home. Setting up your kitchen to support a diabetic renal-friendly lifestyle can transform it into a powerful tool in your health journey. This chapter is dedicated to turning your kitchen into a bastion of wellness, complete with pantry staples and shopping tips to streamline your cooking process while adhering to dietary needs.

5.1 Setting Up Your Diabetic Renal-Friendly Kitchen

Creating a kitchen environment that encourages healthy eating starts with organization and the right tools. Ensure that your kitchen is set up to make meal preparation as straightforward as possible:

Clear Clutter: A well-organized kitchen invites you to cook. Keep counters clear except for essential items and organize your pantry and fridge to make ingredients easily accessible.

Health-Focused Zones: Dedicate areas of your pantry and refrigerator to diabetic renal-friendly foods. Having these items at the forefront makes it easier to choose healthful options.

Invest in Quality Containers: Good storage solutions keep pantry staples fresh and make prepped ingredients readily available for meals.

5.2 Pantry Staples and Shopping Tips

A well-stocked pantry is the backbone of healthful cooking, enabling you to whip up nutritious meals even on the busiest days. Focus on items that are versatile and align with your dietary needs:

Whole Grains: Quinoa, bulgur, and barley are excellent sources of fiber and nutrients, with a lower impact on blood sugar levels.

Low-Sodium Canned Goods: Look for no-salt-added beans, vegetables, and tomatoes to add substance to meals without the extra sodium.

Healthy Oils: Olive and avocado oils are great for cooking and dressing salads, offering heart-healthy fats.

Herbs and Spices: These are essential for flavoring dishes without relying on salt. Stock up on a variety to keep meals interesting.

Nuts and Seeds: Almonds, chia seeds, and flax seeds provide healthy fats and proteins, making great snacks or additions to meals.

Shopping Tips
Shopping with a diabetic renal-friendly diet in mind requires a bit of strategy:

Make a List: Plan your meals for the week and make a shopping list to avoid impulse buys that don't fit your diet.

Read Labels: Always check labels for sodium, sugar, and phosphorus content, especially in packaged and processed foods.

Shop the Perimeter: The outer aisles of the grocery store typically contain the freshest, least processed foods. Make this your primary area to shop.

Seek Out Specialized Stores: Health food stores and farmers' markets can be great sources for organic and less common items that fit into a renal-friendly diet.

Consider Online Subscriptions: For hard-to-find items, online stores can be a valuable resource, often offering bulk purchasing options that can save money in the long run.

Chapter 6:

Recipes for a Vibrant Life

Avocado Toast with Poached Egg

Greek Yogurt with Nuts and Seeds

Oatmeal with Almond Slices

Chicken Salad with Greek Yogurt Dressing

Quinoa Tabbouleh

Vegetable Lentil Soup

Baked Cod with Cherry Tomatoes

Turkey Chili

Eggplant Parmesan

Cucumber and Carrot Sticks with Tzatziki

Roasted Chickpeas

Zucchini Muffins

Peach Cobbler

Almond Joy Chia Pudding

Baked Apples

Berry Smoothie Bowl with Chia Seeds

Cottage Cheese with Pineapple Chunks

Almond Flour Pancakes

Spinach and Feta Stuffed Chicken Breast

Broccoli and Cauliflower Salad

Grilled Shrimp over Mixed Greens

Stuffed Zucchini Boats with Ground Turkey

Baked Trout with Lemon and Dill

Vegetable Stir-Fry with Tofu

Pear Slices with Ricotta Cheese

Edamame with Sea Salt

Pumpkin Seeds and Sunflower Seeds Mix

Coconut Milk Rice Pudding

Dark Chocolate-Dipped Strawberries

Carrot Cake Bites

6.1 Breakfasts to Kickstart Your Day

1.Chia Berry Parfait
Ingredients:
2 tablespoons chia seeds
1/2 cup unsweetened almond milk
1/2 cup mixed berries (fresh or thawed from frozen)
1 tablespoon honey (optional)
A few mint leaves for garnish

Instructions: Mix chia seeds with almond milk and honey (if using) in a glass or jar. Stir well.

Let the mixture sit for at least 4 hours or overnight in the refrigerator until it thickens into a pudding-like consistency.

Layer the chia pudding with mixed berries in a serving glass.

Garnish with mint leaves before serving.

Nutritional Notes: Rich in omega-3 fatty acids from chia seeds, this parfait offers anti-inflammatory benefits, while berries provide antioxidants and a natural sweetness.

2. Spinach and Mushroom Omelet
Ingredients: 2 large eggs
1/2 cup fresh spinach, chopped
1/4 cup mushrooms, sliced
1 tablespoon olive oil
Salt-free seasoning to taste
Optional: 1 tablespoon grated Parmesan cheese

Instructions: In a skillet, heat olive oil over medium heat. Add mushrooms and sauté until browned.

Add spinach and cook until wilted. Remove vegetables from the skillet and set aside.

In a bowl, whisk eggs with a splash of water and salt-free seasoning.

Pour eggs into the skillet, cooking over medium heat. As eggs are set, lift the edges, letting uncooked eggs flow underneath.

When the eggs are almost set, place the sautéed vegetables on one half and fold the omelet over.

Serve hot, garnished with Parmesan cheese if desired.

Nutritional Notes: Eggs provide high-quality protein, essential for muscle maintenance, while spinach offers iron, and mushrooms supply antioxidants.

3. Avocado Toast with Poached Eggs
Ingredients: 1 slice whole-grain bread
1/2 ripe avocado
1 egg

Salt-free seasoning and pepper to taste
Optional: Crushed red pepper flakes

Instructions: Toast the bread to your liking. Spread the avocado on the toast after mashing it. Season with salt-free seasoning and pepper.
Poach the egg in gently simmering water until the white is set but the yolk remains runny for about 3-4 minutes. Using a slotted spoon, remove and let drain on paper towels. Toast with avocado and poached egg on top. If preferred, top with crushed red pepper flakes.

Nutritional Notes: Avocado provides healthy fats for heart health, and eggs are a great protein source, supporting kidney health by being low in phosphorus.

4. Greek Yogurt with Nuts and Seeds
Ingredients: 1 cup plain Greek yogurt
2 tablespoons mixed nuts (almonds, walnuts) and seeds (pumpkin, sunflower)
1 tablespoon honey (optional)

A pinch of cinnamon

Instructions:Spoon the Greek yogurt into a bowl.
Top with mixed nuts and seeds. Drizzle with honey if desired and sprinkle with cinnamon.

Nutritional Notes: Greek yogurt is packed with protein and probiotics for digestive health, while nuts and seeds add essential minerals and healthy fats.

5. Almond Butter Banana Smoothie
Ingredients:1 ripe banana
1 tablespoon almond butter
1 cup unsweetened almond milk
Ice cubes (optional)

Instructions: Place the banana, almond butter, almond milk, and ice cubes (if using) in a blender.
Blend until smooth and creamy.

Nutritional Notes: Bananas offer quick energy and potassium, while almond butter provides healthy fats and protein, making this smoothie a satisfying, kidney-friendly snack.

6. Oatmeal with Almond Slices
Ingredients: 1/2 cup steel-cut oats
1 cup water or almond milk
2 tablespoons almond slices
1 tablespoon honey or maple syrup (optional)
A pinch of cinnamon

Instructions: Cook oats according to package instructions using water or almond milk for added creaminess.
Once cooked, stir in the almond slices. If desired, sweeten with honey or maple syrup. Sprinkle it with cinnamon before serving.

Nutritional Notes: Steel-cut oats are a great source of fiber, aiding in blood sugar control. Almonds add a crunch and healthy fats, enhancing the meal's nutritional profile.

These recipes are designed to be both nutritious and delicious, catering to the dietary

6.2 Nourishing Lunches for Sustained Energy

Cauliflower Rice Stir-Fry

Ingredients:

One cauliflower head, finely chopped into rice-sized chunks

2 tablespoons olive oil

1 cup mixed vegetables (carrots, peas, bell peppers), finely chopped

2 cloves garlic, minced

2 eggs, beaten (optional)

Salt-free seasoning to taste

2 green onions, sliced for garnish

Instructions: In a big skillet over medium heat, warm the olive oil. Add garlic and sauté until fragrant.

Increase heat to medium-high, add mixed vegetables, and stir-fry until just tender.

Add grated cauliflower, mixing thoroughly. Cook for 5-7 minutes, or until cauliflower is tender.
Make a well in the center of the skillet, add beaten eggs, and scramble until fully cooked, mixing with the vegetables.
Season with salt-free seasoning and garnish with green onions.

Nutritional Notes: Cauliflower provides a low-carb, high-fiber alternative to traditional rice, supporting blood sugar management. Vegetables add vitamins and minerals, while eggs offer high-quality protein.

Turkey and Avocado Roll-Ups
Ingredients:
4 slices of turkey breast (low sodium)
1 ripe avocado, sliced
1/2 cucumber, julienned
Salt-free seasoning to taste

Instructions: Lay out turkey slices flat.
Place a few avocado slices and cucumber sticks on each turkey slice.

Season with salt-free seasoning.
Roll up tightly and secure with a toothpick.

Nutritional Notes: This snack is rich in protein from the turkey and healthy fats from the avocado, making it satisfying and heart-healthy.

Lentil Soup
Ingredients:
1 cup dried lentils, rinsed
1 tablespoon olive oil
1 onion, chopped
2 carrots, diced
2 stalks celery, diced
2 cloves garlic, minced
4 cups low-sodium vegetable broth
Salt-free seasoning, thyme, and bay leaf for flavor

Instructions: Heat olive oil in a large pot. Add onion, carrots, celery, and garlic. Sauté until softened.
Add lentils, vegetable broth, seasoning, thyme, and bay leaf.

Bring to a boil, then simmer for 25-30 minutes, or until lentils are tender.
Remove the bay leaf before serving.

Nutritional Notes: Lentils are a great source of plant-based protein and fiber, supporting heart and kidney health by promoting steady blood sugar levels and low blood pressure.

Chicken Salad with Greek Yogurt Dressing
Ingredients:
2 cups cooked chicken breast, shredded
1/2 cup Greek yogurt
1 apple, diced
1/4 cup walnuts, chopped
Salt-free seasoning to taste
Lettuce leaves for serving

Instructions: In a bowl, mix Greek yogurt with salt-free seasoning to make the dressing.
Add shredded chicken, diced apple, and walnuts to the bowl. Mix until well combined.
Serve on a bed of lettuce leaves.

Nutritional Notes: Using Greek yogurt instead of mayonnaise cuts down on unhealthy fats while adding protein. Apples and walnuts provide fiber and healthy fats, respectively.

Quinoa Tabbouleh
Ingredients:
1 cup cooked quinoa, cooled
1 large bunch parsley, finely chopped
1/4 cup fresh mint, chopped
2 tomatoes, diced
1 cucumber, diced
Juice of 1 lemon
2 tablespoons olive oil
Salt-free seasoning to taste

Instructions: In a large bowl, combine quinoa, parsley, mint, tomatoes, and cucumber.
Dress with lemon juice, olive oil, and salt-free seasoning. Mix well.
Before serving, let the flavors settle by chilling for at least thirty minutes.

Nutritional Notes: Quinoa provides complete protein and fiber, making this dish filling and nutritious. The herbs and vegetables contribute vitamins and antioxidants.

Vegetable Lentil Soup
Ingredients: Follow the Lentil Soup recipe, adding 1 cup of diced tomatoes and 1 cup of chopped spinach or kale for extra nutrients and flavor.

Instructions: Follow the same steps as the Lentil Soup recipe, adding the tomatoes with the lentils and the leafy greens about 5 minutes before the end of cooking to keep them vibrant and tender.

Nutritional Notes: The addition of tomatoes adds lycopene, an antioxidant, and leafy greens contribute iron and additional fiber, enhancing the soup's nutritional profile.

6.3 Satisfying Dinners That Delight

Grilled Lemon-Garlic Salmon
Ingredients:
4 salmon filets (4-6 oz each)
2 tablespoons olive oil
2 cloves garlic, minced
Juice and zest of 1 lemon
Salt-free herb seasoning

Instructions:
Preheat the grill to medium-high heat.
In a bowl, whisk together olive oil, garlic, lemon juice, zest, and seasoning.
Brush salmon filets with the lemon-garlic mixture.
Grill salmon, skin-side down, for 6-8 minutes or until done to your liking.

Nutritional Notes: Salmon is rich in omega-3 fatty acids, beneficial for heart health. This recipe uses heart-healthy olive oil and lemon for flavor, avoiding added sodium.

Beef Stir-Fry

Ingredients:

1 lb lean beef, thinly sliced

2 cups mixed vegetables (broccoli, bell peppers, and carrots)

2 tablespoons olive oil

2 cloves garlic, minced

1 tablespoon low-sodium soy sauce

Salt-free seasoning

Instructions:

In a large skillet set over medium-high heat, warm the olive oil. Add garlic and beef slices, stir-frying until browned.

Add vegetables and continue to stir-fry until just tender.

Stir in low-sodium soy sauce and seasoning, cooking for an additional minute.

Nutritional Notes: Lean beef provides high-quality protein. Opting for low-sodium soy sauce and salt-free seasonings helps manage sodium intake.

Stuffed Bell Peppers

Ingredients:
4 large bell peppers, halved and seeded
1 lb ground turkey
1 cup cooked quinoa
1 cup diced tomatoes
1 onion, diced
2 cloves garlic, minced
Salt-free Italian seasoning

Instructions:
Preheat the oven to 375°F (190°C).
Cook the turkey, onion, and garlic in a skillet until the turkey is browned. Stir in quinoa, tomatoes, and seasoning.
Stuffed bell pepper halves with the turkey mixture. Cover with foil and place in a baking dish. Bake the peppers for thirty minutes, or until they are soft.

Nutritional Notes: This dish is high in protein and fiber, with quinoa providing a complete protein source and bell peppers adding vitamins and antioxidants.

Baked Cod with Cherry Tomatoes

Ingredients:
4 cod filets
2 cups cherry tomatoes
2 tablespoons olive oil
Juice of 1 lemon
Salt-free seasoning

Instructions:
Preheat the oven to 400°F (200°C).
Place cod filets in a baking dish. Surround with cherry tomatoes.
Pour in some lemon juice and olive oil.
Bake for 12-15 minutes, until cod is cooked through.

Nutritional Notes: Cod is a low-fat protein source, making it suitable for a renal diet. Tomatoes provide vitamin C and lycopene, while olive oil offers healthy fats.

Turkey Chili
Ingredients:
1 lb ground turkey
2 cans of low-sodium diced tomatoes
1 can low-sodium kidney beans, rinsed

1 onion, diced
2 cloves garlic, minced
1 tablespoon chili powder
Salt-free seasoning

Instructions:
In a large pot, cook turkey, onion, and garlic over medium heat until the turkey is browned.
Add tomatoes, beans, chili powder, and seasoning, and stir well.
Simmer for 20 to 30 minutes to let the flavors combine.

Nutritional Notes: Using ground turkey instead of beef reduces saturated fat intake. Low-sodium canned goods help manage kidney health.

Eggplant Parmesan
Ingredients:
1/2-inch circles cut from 2 large eggplants
2 cups low-sodium marinara sauce
1 cup shredded mozzarella cheese
1/2 cup grated Parmesan cheese

Salt-free Italian seasoning

Instructions:
Preheat the oven to 375°F (190°C).
Layer a baking dish with a bit of marinara sauce. Arrange a layer of eggplant slices, top with more sauce, and sprinkle with mozzarella and Parmesan. Repeat layers.
Cover with foil and bake for 25 minutes. Remove foil and bake for another 10 minutes until cheese is bubbly.

Nutritional Notes: Eggplant is a great source of fiber and antioxidants. Choosing low-sodium marinara sauce and limiting cheese helps control sodium and phosphorus intake.

6.4 Snacks and Sides: Your Allies in Health

Veggie Sticks with Hummus
Ingredients:
1 cup hummus (store-bought or homemade)

Variety of raw vegetables (carrots, celery, bell peppers, and cucumber), cut into sticks

Instructions:
Prepare a colorful assortment of raw vegetables by washing and cutting them into stick shapes.
Serve the vegetable sticks with a bowl of hummus for dipping.

Nutritional Notes: This snack is rich in fiber from the vegetables and protein from the hummus, making it an ideal choice for maintaining blood sugar levels and kidney health.

Apple Slices with Nut Butter
Ingredients:
1 apple, cored and sliced
2 tablespoons of almond butter or peanut butter

Instructions:
Core and slice the apple into thin pieces.

Spread nut butter over each slice before serving.

Nutritional Notes: Apples are a great source of fiber and antioxidants, while nut butter provides healthy fats and protein, contributing to heart health and satiety.

Berry Sorbet
Ingredients:
2 cups frozen mixed berries
2 tablespoons honey or agave syrup (optional)
Juice of 1 lemon

Instructions:
Blend the frozen berries, sweetener (if using), and lemon juice in a food processor or blender until smooth.
Serve immediately for a soft texture, or freeze for 1-2 hours for a firmer sorbet.

Nutritional Notes: Berries are low in calories and high in antioxidants, making this dessert not only refreshing but also beneficial for overall health.

Cucumber Carrot Sticks with Tzatziki
Ingredients:
1/2 cucumber, diced
1 cup Greek yogurt
1 clove garlic, minced
1 tablespoon dill, chopped
Juice of 1/2 lemon
Salt-free seasoning to taste
Carrot and cucumber sticks for serving

Instructions:
To make the tzatziki, combine Greek yogurt, diced cucumber, minced garlic, dill, lemon juice, and seasoning in a bowl. Mix well.
Chill in the refrigerator for at least 30 minutes before serving with carrot and cucumber sticks.

Nutritional Notes: Tzatziki is a protein-rich dip thanks to Greek yogurt, and when paired with vegetable sticks, it makes for a hydrating and nutritious snack.

Zucchini Muffins

Ingredients:

1 1/2 cups whole wheat flour

1/2 cup unsweetened apple sauce

1/4 cup honey or maple syrup

1 teaspoon baking soda

1/2 teaspoon salt-free spice blend

1 cup grated zucchini (water squeezed out)

2 eggs, beaten

1 teaspoon vanilla extract

Instructions:

Preheat your oven to 350°F (175°C) and prepare a muffin tin with liners or a light coating of oil.

Mix the flour, baking soda, and spice blend in a large bowl.

In a separate bowl, combine the apple sauce, honey, eggs, and vanilla. Stir in the zucchini. Combine the wet and dry ingredients, stirring until just mixed.

Fill the muffin tins and bake for 20-25 minutes, or until a toothpick comes out clean.

Nutritional Notes: These muffins offer a sneaky way to include vegetables in your diet. Zucchini provides vitamins and fiber while using whole wheat flour and unsweetened applesauce boosts the fiber content and reduces added sugars.

6.5 Sweet Treats: Guilt-Free Pleasures

Cinnamon Baked Pears
Ingredients:
4 ripe pears, halved and cored
2 tablespoons honey
1/2 teaspoon ground cinnamon
1/4 cup walnuts, chopped

Instructions:
Preheat your oven to 350°F (175°C).
Place the pear halves on a baking dish, and cut the side up.
Drizzle with honey and sprinkle cinnamon
Bake for 25-30 minutes, or until the pears are soft and juicy.

Garnish with chopped walnuts before serving.

Nutritional Notes: Pears are rich in fiber and essential antioxidants. The cinnamon not only adds flavor but also has blood sugar-regulating properties

Avocado Chocolate Mousse
Ingredients:
2 ripe avocados, peeled and pitted
1/4 cup cocoa powder
1/4 cup honey or maple syrup
1 teaspoon vanilla extract
A pinch of salt

Instructions:
Blend or process all ingredients in a food processor until smooth. Before serving, let the mousse cool for at least an hour in the refrigerator. Serve with a garnish of fresh raspberries or shaved dark chocolate.

Nutritional Notes: Avocado provides heart-healthy fats, while cocoa adds antioxidants without the added fat of traditional chocolate desserts.

Peach Cobbler
Ingredients:
4 cups sliced fresh peaches
1/4 cup honey
1 cup whole wheat flour
1/4 cup unsalted butter, melted
1/2 cup milk (almond milk for a dairy-free option)
1 teaspoon baking powder
1/4 teaspoon salt

Instructions:
Preheat your oven to 375°F (190°C).
Arrange the peach slices in a baking dish and drizzle with half the honey.
In a bowl, mix the flour, baking powder, salt, melted butter, milk, and the remaining honey to form a batter.
Pour the batter over the peaches, spreading evenly.

Bake until the topping is brown, 35 to 40 minutes. Serve warm, optionally with a dollop of Greek yogurt.

Nutritional Notes: Peaches are low in calories but high in vitamins A and C. Whole wheat flour increases fiber content, making this dessert a healthier option.

Almond Joy Chia Pudding
Ingredients:
1/4 cup chia seeds
1 cup unsweetened almond milk
2 tablespoons cocoa powder
2 tablespoons honey or maple syrup
1/4 teaspoon almond extract
2 tablespoons shredded coconut
2 tablespoons chopped almonds

Instructions:
In a jar, combine chia seeds, almond milk, cocoa powder, honey, and almond extract. Stir well.
Refrigerate for at least 4 hours or overnight, until it has thickened.

Before serving, stir in shredded coconut and top with chopped almonds.

Nutritional Notes: Chia seeds are a fantastic source of omega-3 fatty acids and fiber. Cocoa powder adds flavor and antioxidants without excess sugar.

Baked Apples
Ingredients:
4 large apples, cored
1/4 cup chopped walnuts
1/4 cup dried cranberries
2 tablespoons honey
1/2 teaspoon ground cinnamon

Instructions:
Preheat your oven to 350°F (175°C).
Mix walnuts, cranberries, honey, and cinnamon in a bowl.
Stuff the apples with the mixture and place them in a baking dish.
Fill the dish with just enough water to cover the bottom. Bake for thirty to forty minutes, or until the apples are soft. Serve warm,

perhaps with a side of whipped cream or Greek yogurt.

Nutritional Notes: This dessert is high in fiber from the apples and contains healthy fats from the walnuts. Cinnamon and honey add natural sweetness and flavor, making this a guilt-free treat.

Chapter 7:

Living the Diabetic Renal Diet

Embracing a diabetic renal diet is more than following a list of food dos and don'ts it's about transforming your lifestyle to improve your health and well-being. Let's explore how to adapt to these dietary changes with ease and confidence and how to navigate dining out and attending social events.

7.1 Adapting to Dietary Changes with Ease and Confidence

Start with a clear understanding of why certain foods are recommended or restricted. Knowledge is power, and understanding the impact of food choices on your blood sugar and kidney health can motivate you to make healthier decisions.

Meal Planning: Plan your meals ahead of time. This not only helps in adhering to your diet but also reduces the stress of last-minute decisions. Incorporate a variety of foods within your dietary guidelines to keep meals interesting and nutritious.

Cooking at Home: Embrace cooking at home as it allows you to control ingredients, portions, and cooking methods. Experiment with herbs and spices to add flavor without salt or sugar. Cooking can become a creative and enjoyable part of your day.
Support System: Build a support system of family and friends who understand your dietary needs. Sharing your journey can provide encouragement and accountability.

Educating Yourself: Continuously educate yourself on the diabetic renal diet. Resources like books, websites, and support groups can offer new insights and recipes to try.

7.2 Dining Out: Navigating Restaurants and Social

EventsRestaurant Choices: Choose restaurants that offer flexibility in their menu that can accommodate your dietary needs. Many places are willing to modify dishes by leaving out certain ingredients like salt or sugar.

Menu Research: Before visiting a restaurant, look at the menu online to plan what to order. Knowing what's safe to eat ahead of time can ease anxiety and make dining out enjoyable.

Communicate Your Needs: Don't hesitate to communicate your dietary restrictions to the server or chef. Most restaurants are accustomed to accommodating special dietary requests.

Portion Control: Restaurant portions can be larger than what you're used to. Consider sharing a dish or asking for half of it to be packed to go.

Social Events: For social events, consider eating a small, renal-friendly meal before you go. This can help curb hunger and make it easier to avoid temptation. Alternatively, offer to bring a dish to share that fits your dietary needs.

Beverage Choices: Pay attention to your drink choices. Opt for water, unsweetened tea, or other beverages that align with your dietary guidelines.

Living with a diabetic renal diet is a journey of adaptation and learning. By planning, making informed choices, and seeking support, you can navigate this lifestyle confidently, enjoying a variety of nutritious and delicious foods while managing your health. Remember, your diet doesn't have to be restrictive it's an opportunity to discover new foods and flavors that benefit your body and soul.

Chapter 8:

Beyond the Diet

Adopting a diabetic renal diet is a significant step towards better health, but it's just one part of a holistic approach to managing your condition. Incorporating physical activity, managing stress, and ensuring regular medical check-ups are also vital components of a comprehensive health strategy.

8.1 Incorporating Physical Activity into Your Routine

Find What You Enjoy: The key to sustained physical activity is finding exercises you enjoy. Whether it's walking, swimming, cycling, or yoga, engaging in activities that bring you joy will make it easier to stick with them.

Set Realistic Goals: Start with achievable goals, such as a 15-minute walk each day, gradually increasing intensity and duration. Celebrate your milestones to stay motivated.

Incorporate Variety: Keep your routine interesting by mixing different types of activities. This keeps you from becoming bored while also working different muscle groups and enhancing your general health.

Listen to Your Body: Be Aware of the Cues Your Body Sends Out. On days you feel tired, consider gentler activities like stretching or leisurely walks. Remember, rest is also a crucial part of your fitness journey.

8.2 Stress Management and Mental Well-being

Mindfulness and Meditation: Practices like mindfulness and meditation can significantly reduce stress levels, improving both mental and physical health. You can make an impact with just a few minutes each day.

Connect with Others: Building and maintaining social connections can provide emotional support and reduce feelings of isolation. To share experiences and suggestions, think about joining support groups.

Hobbies and Interests: Engage in hobbies and activities that relax and fulfill you. Whether it's reading, gardening, painting, or playing music, these activities can provide a helpful distraction from stress.

Seek Professional Help: If you find stress and anxiety difficult to manage, don't hesitate to seek help from a mental health professional. Therapy can provide useful coping mechanisms for stressful situations.

8.3 The Importance of Regular Check-ups and Monitoring

Stay on Top of Your Health: Regular check-ups with your healthcare team are crucial for monitoring your condition and adjusting your treatment plan as needed. Be proactive in scheduling appointments and screenings.

Keep Records: Maintain a health journal detailing your blood sugar levels, blood pressure, kidney function tests, and any symptoms or changes you notice. This record can be invaluable for your healthcare provider in managing your health.

Medication Management: If you're on medication, take it as prescribed and discuss any side effects with your doctor. Regular review of your medications can ensure they're still effective and necessary.

Educate Yourself: Stay informed about your condition. Understanding the latest research and treatment options can empower you to make informed decisions about your health.

Chapter 9:

Troubleshooting Common Challenge

Adhering to a diabetic renal diet, like any significant lifestyle change, comes with its set of challenges. Navigating dietary slip-ups and managing cravings are among the hurdles you might encounter. Let's explore strategies to overcome these obstacles, ensuring a smoother journey towards health and wellness.

9.1 Managing Dietary Slip-Ups

Acceptance and Compassion: Understand that slip-ups are a natural part of any lifestyle change. Approach these moments with self-compassion rather than criticism. Acknowledge the slip-up, learn from it, and move forward.

Identify Triggers: Reflect on what led to the slip-up. Was it a specific event, emotion, or perhaps a lack of preparation? Identifying triggers can help you develop strategies to avoid similar situations in the future.

Create a Plan: Once you've identified potential triggers, create a plan. This could involve meal planning, having healthy snacks on hand, or finding stress-reduction techniques that work for you.

Seek Support: Don't hesitate to seek support from friends, family, or healthcare professionals. Sharing your experiences can provide you with encouragement and accountability.

9.2 Dealing with Cravings and Dietary Restrictions

Healthy Alternatives: For every craving, there's often a healthier alternative that can satisfy you without derailing your diet. Craving something sweet? Try fresh fruit with a sprinkle of cinnamon. Salty? A few olives or pickles can be satisfying.

Mindful Eating: Practice mindful eating by paying full attention to the experience of eating and savoring your food. This practice can help you enjoy your meals more fully and feel satisfied with lcss.

Balance and Moderation: It's okay to indulge occasionally. The key is moderation. Allowing yourself a small portion of a carved item can prevent feelings of deprivation, making it easier to stick to your dietary plan in the long run.

Educate Yourself: Knowledge is power. Educating yourself about the nutritional content of foods can help you make informed decisions that align with your cravings without compromising your health goals.

Focus on What You Can Have: Instead of dwelling on restrictions, focus on the variety of foods you can enjoy. Exploring new recipes and flavors can make your dietary journey exciting and fulfilling.

Appendices

Navigating a diabetic renal diet, particularly when managing food allergies or seeking further education, can feel overwhelming. These appendices are designed to support and enrich your journey toward health and wellness.

Appendix A: Substitute Ingredients for Common Allergens

Dairy: Replace cow's milk with almond, coconut, or oat milk. For cheese, nutritional yeast or dairy-free cheese alternatives can offer a similar flavor profile.

Nuts: Seeds, like sunflower or pumpkin seeds, can be a great alternative for nut allergies. For nut butter, sunflower seed butter or tahini.

Gluten: Choose gluten-free grains such as quinoa, rice, or certified gluten-free oats. Gluten-free flours like almond or coconut flour can substitute for wheat flour in recipes.

Eggs: For baking, use flaxseed or chia seed meal mixed with water as a binding substitute. Applesauce or mashed banana can also replace eggs in some recipes.

Soy: Coconut aminos can replace soy sauce for those avoiding soy. For tofu, consider chickpea-based alternatives or simply increase your intake of other legumes.

Appendix B: Weekly Meal Planner Template

Monday

Breakfast: Avocado Toast with Poached Egg Whole-grain bread, mashed avocado, poached egg, topped with fresh dill.

Lunch: Turkey and Spinach Salad

Mixed greens, sliced turkey breast, spinach, cherry tomatoes, and cucumber with olive oil and lemon dressing.

Dinner: Grilled Chicken with Quinoa and Steamed Broccoli
Grilled chicken breast seasoned with herbs, served with cooked quinoa and a side of steamed broccoli.

Snacks: Carrot Sticks with Hummus; Greek Yogurt with Blueberries.

Tuesday

Breakfast: Berry and Chia Smoothie
Blend unsweetened almond milk, mixed berries, chia seeds, and a touch of honey.

Lunch: Vegetable Stir-Fry with Tofu
Stir-fried bell peppers, bok choy, carrots, and tofu in a low-sodium soy sauce, served over brown rice.

Dinner: Baked Salmon with Asparagus.

Oven-baked salmon with lemon slices served with roasted asparagus.

Snacks: Apple Slices with Almond Butter; Cucumber Slices.

Wednesday

Breakfast: Oatmeal with Almond Slices and Cinnamon.
Steel-cut oats cooked with water, topped with almond slices, cinnamon, and a drizzle of maple syrup.

Lunch: Chicken Caesar Salad
Romaine lettuce, grilled chicken strips, a sprinkle of Parmesan cheese, and a light Caesar dressing (anchovies optional).

Dinner: Beef Stir-Fry
Lean beef strips stir-fried with broccoli, snap peas, and bell peppers, seasoned with ginger, and served over quinoa.

Snacks: A handful of Mixed Nuts; Sliced Peaches

Thursday

Breakfast: Greek Yogurt Parfait
Layers of Greek yogurt, granola (low-sugar), and mixed berries.

Lunch: Lentil Soup
Lentils cooked with carrots, celery, tomatoes, and low-sodium broth, seasoned with thyme.

Dinner: Roasted Turkey Breast with Sweet Potatoes
Oven-roasted turkey breast served with baked sweet potatoes and green beans.

Snacks: Edamame; Cottage Cheese with Pineapple

Friday

Breakfast: Scrambled Eggs with Sautéed Spinach
Eggs scrambled with olive oil, garlic, and spinach, served on whole-grain toast.

Lunch: Quinoa Salad
Quinoa mixed with black beans, corn, avocado, lime juice, and cilantro.

Dinner: Grilled Shrimp Tacos
Grilled shrimp served in corn tortillas with cabbage slaw and avocado slices.

Snacks: Pear Slices; Bell Pepper Strips with Guacamole.

Saturday

Breakfast: Banana Nut Muffins
Whole-grain banana muffins with walnuts.

Lunch: Turkey Wrap
Whole-grain wrap filled with turkey breast, lettuce, tomato, and mustard.

Dinner: Stuffed Bell Peppers
Bell peppers stuffed with a mixture of ground turkey, brown rice, diced tomatoes, and Italian herbs.

Snacks: Greek Yogurt with Honey; Raw Veggies with Ranch Dip (low sodium)

Sunday

Breakfast: Smoothie Bowl
A smoothie bowl made with spinach, banana, and almond milk, topped with granola, coconut, and fresh fruit.

Lunch: Caprese Salad
Slices of fresh tomato and mozzarella cheese, topped with basil leaves and balsamic glaze.

Dinner: Lemon Garlic Pasta with Grilled Vegetables
Whole-grain pasta tossed in a lemon garlic sauce served with grilled zucchini and eggplant.

Snacks: Hard-Boiled Eggs; Mixed Berries.

(Continue for each day of the week)
Notes: Include any dietary considerations or allergen substitutes needed for each meal. Plan for leftovers to minimize food waste and simplify meal preparation.

Appendix C: Glossary of Terms

Diabetic Renal Diet: A diet plan designed to manage blood sugar levels and reduce strain on the kidneys, typically low in sodium, phosphorus, and certain proteins.

Glycemic Index: A measure of how quickly foods cause increases in blood glucose levels.

Phosphorus: A mineral found in many foods, managed in a renal diet to prevent bone and cardiovascular issues.

Potassium: An essential mineral regulated in kidney-friendly diets to maintain heart and muscle function.

Sodium: Commonly found in salt, this mineral is limited in a renal diet to manage blood pressure and prevent fluid retention.

Appendix D: Additional Resources for Continued Learning

"Eating Well for Kidney Health" by Helena Jackson

MyFitnessPal: For tracking meals and nutritional content.

Kidney Kitchen: Offers kidney-friendly recipes and meal-planning tips.

Printed in Great Britain
by Amazon

42309484R00050